Pope John Paul II

HIS ESSENTIAL WISDOM

EDITED BY

CAROL KELLY-GANGI

BARNES & NOBLE

NEW YORK

To Mom and Dad with love—
for your lifelong example of faith.

The editor wishes to extend a special thanks to Gwen and Howard Kelly, Marianne Kelly, and Beverly Lindh for all of their efforts and support, and especially to Barbara Kelly-Vergona for her valuable contributions.

The quotes in this book have been drawn from many sources, and are assumed to be accurate as quoted in their previously published forms. Although every effort has been made to verify the quotes and sources, the publisher cannot guarantee their perfect accuracy.

2005 Barnes & Noble Books

ISBN 0-7607-7798-5

Printed and bound in the United States of America

05 06 07 08 09 HC 9 8 7 6 5 4 3 2 1

Introduction

ON OCTOBER 16, 1978, WHEN KAROL WOJTYLA was elected pope, he gave his first address to the audience and declared that he had been called from a far-away country. Indeed, many in the crowd who had been anxiously awaiting news of the newly elected pope were, upon hearing Wojtyla's name, unsure of exactly who he was. Few on that day could have imagined that this kind-faced man from Poland would vigorously lead the world's more than one billion Catholics for close to twenty-seven years, into the third millennium, and become the third longest serving pope in the history of the Catholic Church.

From his humble beginnings in the town of Wadowice, Poland, Karol Wojtyla had lived through tremendous personal loss. His mother died when he was nine years old, and his older brother succumbed to scarlet fever only three years later. In 1941, when Karol was not yet twenty-one, his beloved father died, leaving the young man to find his own way in the world. Up until that time, his passion in life had been the theater, acting, and literature. But the horrors of the war and the devastating losses he had suffered paved the way for Karol's vocation.

From his ordination to the priesthood in 1946, Wojtyla began his meteoric rise in the Catholic Church. Studying in Rome and at the Jagiellonian University in Kraków, he was awarded two doctorate degrees, and he taught standing-room only courses in philosophy and ethics at the Catholic University of Lublin. In 1958, Wojtyla was named auxiliary bishop of Kraków by Pope Pius XII; at thirty-eight years of age, he was the youngest bishop in Poland. He was named Archbishop of Kraków by Pope Paul VI in 1963. And after his key participation in all four sessions of Vatican II, Wojtyla was made a cardinal by Pope Paul VI in 1967.

From the beginning of his papacy, Pope John Paul II embraced his mission to bring the message of Christ to the world. He criss-crossed the globe and made an astounding 104 trips abroad despite failing health in the last decade of his life. During his travels, he spoke to and connected with millions of people in venues as diverse as cathedrals, universities, mosques, baseball stadiums, racetracks, and airports. Whether on his travels, at the Vatican, or on holiday, Pope John Paul II remained deeply committed to prayer. He devot-ed time to prayer every day, and viewed each person he met as some-one entrusted to him by Christ. In 1981, he survived an assassination attempt, and later met with his would-be assassin in prison and offered his forgiveness. He had a special relationship with the youth of the world. In 1984, he established World Youth Day, which became a recurring event where millions of young people gathered together to hear the words of the Holy Father and to celebrate their faith.

A champion of ecumenism, Pope John Paul II worked tirelessly to find common ground among Christians of different sects as well as with the other world religions, particularly with Judaism and Islam. He was the first modern pope to visit a synagogue, the first to visit Auschwitz concentration camp, and in an historic trip to Jerusalem in 2000, he prayed at the Western Wall, and placed a prayer there for forgiveness. In fact, during the course of his pontificate, Pope John Paul II made public apologies for more than one hundred wrongs committed by the Catholic Church throughout its history. He lobbied continually for peace, was instrumental in the fall of the "iron curtain," and a tireless advocate for the poor, leading a successful campaign for global debt relief as part of the Jubilee Year 2000.

Despite criticism, Pope John Paul II remained steadfast in professing his beliefs. He was uncompromising in his commitment to human life. He viewed abortion, capital punishment, and euthanasia as a part of what he called "the culture of death" that permeated life in the modern world, and he warned against the dangers of unrestrained materialism and consumerism.

This book offers readers hundreds of quotations from Pope John Paul II. In these excerpts, he speaks passionately about the message of Christ, the quest for social justice, the importance of family, the meaning of suffering, the power of prayer, the way to peace, and the dignity and equality of every human being. In other selections, Pope John Paul II vividly recalls his early years, life in war-torn Poland, and his call to serve God.

When Pope John Paul II died on April 2, 2005, the world stopped to mourn. World leaders and dignitaries—Christian and non-Christian alike—joined to express their condolences. More than four million people traveled to Vatican City for the public viewing of his body in St. Peter's Basilica, amounting to one of the largest pilgrimages in the history of Christianity. Pope John Paul II had completed his journey. He came from a far-away country, and in the course of his remarkable life and pontificate, left an indelible mark on the Catholic Church and on the world. Perhaps Pope Benedict XVI, in his first papal message, spoke the words that all the world wanted to hear and that were at the heart of Pope John Paul II's ministry when he said, "It seems I can feel his strong hand squeezing mine; I seem to see his smiling eyes and listen to his words, addressed to me especially at this moment: 'Do not be afraid!'"

Carol Kelly-Gangi
Rumson, New Jersey, 2005

Early Years

You'll see, my Lolek will be a great man someday.

EMILIA WOJTYLA, TO A NEIGHBOR
ABOUT HER INFANT SON, KAROL

I remember as though it were yesterday when, together with the other boys and girls of my own age, I received the Eucharist for the first time in the parish church of my town. This event is usually commemorated in a family photo, so that it will not be forgotten. Photos like these generally remain with a person all through his or her life. As time goes by, people take out these pictures and experience once more the emotions of those moments; they return to the purity and joy experienced in the meeting with Jesus, the One who out of love became the Redeemer of man.

LETTER OF THE POPE TO CHILDREN, 1994

As children we all waited for Saint Nicholas to bring us presents. . . . He distinguished himself as a bishop by his great concern for the poor and needy. I remember that as a child I had a personal devotion to him. Naturally, like every other child, I looked forward to the gifts he would bring me on December sixth. But this expectation had a religious dimension too. Like my peers, I felt a certain veneration toward this saint who unselfishly lavished gifts upon the people, thereby demonstrating his loving concern for them.

RISE, LET US BE ON OUR WAY

From my earliest childhood I have loved books. It was my father who introduced me to reading. . . . After my mother died, the two of us remained alone. He continued to encourage me to explore good literature and he never stood in the way of my interest in the theater. But for the outbreak of war and the radical change that it brought, maybe the prospects opening up for me through academic study would have absorbed me completely.

RISE, LET US BE ON OUR WAY

My preparation for the priesthood in the seminary was *in a certain sense* preceded by the preparation I received *in my family*, thanks to the life and example of my parents. Above all I am grateful to *my father*, who became a widower at an early age.... Day after day I was able to observe the austere way in which he lived. By profession he was a soldier and, after my mother's death, his life became one of constant prayer. Sometimes I would wake up during the night and find my father on his knees, just as I would always see him kneeling in the parish church. We never spoke about a vocation to the priesthood, but *his example was in a way my first seminary*, a kind of domestic seminary.

GIFT AND MYSTERY

At twenty, I had already lost all the people I loved and even the ones that I might have loved, such as the big sister who had died, so I was told, six years before my birth. I was not old enough to make my first communion when I lost my mother, who did not have the happiness of seeing the day to which she looked forward as a great day....

BE NOT AFRAID!

A Call to Serve

After my father's death, which occurred in February 1941, I gradually became aware of my true path. I was working at the factory and devoting myself, as far as the terrors of the occupation allowed, to my taste for literature and drama. My priestly vocation took shape in the midst of all that, like an inner fact of unquestionable and absolute clarity. The following year, in the autumn, I knew that I was called. I could see clearly what I had to give up and the goal that I had to attain, "without a backward glance." I would be a priest.

BE NOT AFRAID!

I was spared much of the immense and horrible drama of the Second World War. I could have been arrested any day, at home, in the stone quarry, in the plant, and taken away to a concentration camp. Sometimes I would ask myself: so many young people of my own age are losing their lives, *why not me?* Today I know that it was not mere chance. Amid the overwhelming evil of the war, everything in my own personal life was tending towards the good of my vocation.

GIFT AND MYSTERY

The tragedy of the war had its effect on my gradual choice of a vocation. It helped me to understand in a new way *the value and importance of a vocation.* In the face of the spread of evil and the atrocities of the war, the meaning of the priesthood and its mission in the world became much clearer to me.

GIFT AND MYSTERY

As for me, from the very first years of my priesthood, the celebration of the Eucharist has been not only my most sacred duty, but above all my soul's deepest need.

GIFT AND MYSTERY

In my reading and in my studies I always tried to achieve a harmony between faith, reason, and the heart. These are not separate areas, but are profoundly interconnected, each giving life to the other.

RISE, LET US BE ON OUR WAY

How alive is in my memory my first encounter with the Eternal City. It was late autumn 1946, when, after I was ordained as priest, I arrived here to continue my studies. . . . I carried in me the image of Rome from history, from literature and from the entire Christian tradition. For many days, I crisscrossed the city, which then had one million inhabitants, and I couldn't fully find the image of that Rome I had brought with me. Slowly, slowly, I found it. It came to me especially after touring the catacombs. . . .

POPE JOHN PAUL II, FROM POPE JOHN
PAUL II: THE BIOGRAPHY BY TAD SZULC

As I entered the office of the Primate, he told me that the Holy Father had named me an auxiliary bishop to the archbishop of Kraków. . . . Upon hearing the words of the Primate informing me of the decision of the Holy See, I said, "Your Eminence, I am too young; I'm only thirty-eight." But the Primate said, "That is a weakness which can soon be remedied. Please do not oppose the will of the Holy Father." So I said, "I accept."

RISE, LET US BE ON OUR WAY

The ring on the bishop's finger signifies that he is married to the Church. . . . This ring, a nuptial symbol, expresses the particular bond between the bishop and the Church. For me it is a daily call to fidelity. It is like a silent question that echoes in my conscience: Am I totally dedicated to my Bride—the Church? Am I sufficiently "for" the communities, families, young and old people, and also "for" those yet to be born?

RISE, LET US BE ON OUR WAY

A New Pope

I think that the conclave's vote that day surprised many people besides me! But what God commands, which may seem humanly impossible, he gives us the means to carry out. That is the secret of every vocation. Every vocation changes our plans, disclosing a new one, and it is astonishing to see how much inner help God gives us, how he tunes us in to a new "wave length," how he prepares us to enter into this new plan and to make it our own by simply seeing it as the Father's will and accepting it. And all this whatever our weakness and our attachment to our personal views.

BE NOT AFRAID!

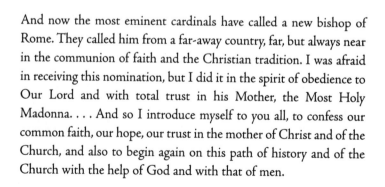

And now the most eminent cardinals have called a new bishop of Rome. They called him from a far-away country, far, but always near in the communion of faith and the Christian tradition. I was afraid in receiving this nomination, but I did it in the spirit of obedience to Our Lord and with total trust in his Mother, the Most Holy Madonna. . . . And so I introduce myself to you all, to confess our common faith, our hope, our trust in the mother of Christ and of the Church, and also to begin again on this path of history and of the Church with the help of God and with that of men.

POPE JOHN PAUL II'S FIRST ADDRESS, ST. PETER'S BASILICA, ROME, OCTOBER 16, 1978

To all people of today, I once again repeat the impassioned cry with which I began my pastoral ministry: "Do not be afraid! Open, indeed, open wide the doors to Christ!" Open to his saving power the confines of states, and systems political and economic, as well as the vast fields of culture, civilization, and development. Do not be afraid. Christ knows "what is inside a person." Only he knows! Today too often people do not know what they carry inside, in the deepest recesses of their soul, in their heart. Too often people are uncertain about a sense of life on earth. Invaded by doubts they are led into despair. Therefore—with humility and trust I beg and implore you—allow Christ to speak to the person in you. Only he has the words of life, yes, eternal life.

HOMILY AT POPE JOHN PAUL II'S
INSTALLATION MASS, OCTOBER 22, 1978

It is not easy to give up the return to the Motherland. . . . But I ask you to oppose everything that violates human dignity and diminishes the habits of a healthy society, often threatening its very existence. . . . My Beloved Countrymen: whenever you receive the blessing of Pope John Paul II, remember that he came from among you and that he has a special right to your hearts and your prayers. . . .

MESSAGE OF POPE JOHN PAUL II TO
POLISH PEOPLE ENTITLED "MY BELOVED
COUNTRYMEN," OCTOBER 23, 1978

Dear Lusia:

God has decreed that I remain in Rome. It is indeed an unusual edict of Holy Providence. These days I think a lot of my parents and of [my brother] Mundek, but I also think of your mother and father, who were always so good to me. . . .You are the only one left living of all my closest family. . . .

LETTER TO HIS COUSIN, FELICJA, IN
JOHN PAUL II'S SECOND WEEK AS
POPE, OCTOBER, 1978

I am constantly aware that in everything I say and do in fulfillment of my vocation, my mission, my ministry, what happens is not just my own initiative. I know that it is not I alone who act in what I do as the successor of Peter.

MEMORY AND IDENTITY

God the Father, the Son, and the Holy Spirit

At the heart of every culture lies the attitude man takes to the greatest mystery: the mystery of God. Different cultures are basically different ways of facing the question of the meaning of personal existence.

CENTESIMUS ANNUS, 1991

Yes, God alone is our true and unfailing support, just as love and prayer are the only sure spiritual levers with which it is possible to lift up the world. And this applies to all areas of life.

ANGELUS PRAYER, SIRACUSA, SICILY, 1994

I am not severe—I am sweet by nature—but I defend the rigidity principle. God is stronger than human weakness and deviations. God will always have the last word.

HOMILY AT SUBURBAN CHURCH, ROME

Christianity can never be reduced to a set of rules and regulations; it is above all a person, Jesus Christ, perfect God and perfect man. It was he who told the Prince of the Apostles, "You are Peter, and upon this rock, I will build my Church, and the gates of hell will not prevail against it." Those are the tremendous claims of Catholicism: that God became man and that he founded his Church on the shoulders of a poor fisherman.

ADDRESS, CARACAS, VENEZUELA, 1985

Jesus came to meet men and women, to heal the sick and the suffering, to free those possessed by devils and to raise the dead. He gave himself on the cross and rose again from the dead, revealing that he is the Lord of life—the author and the source of life without end.

MESSAGE IN PREPARATION FOR
EIGHTH WORLD YOUTH DAY, 1992

In this Jubilee year, we too *have set out to meet Christ*, the Redeemer of man. In passing through the Holy Door, we have experienced his mysterious presence, through which man was given the possibility of passing from sin to grace, from death to life. The Son of God, who became flesh for us, has made us feel the powerful call to conversion and love.

HOMILY AT MASS FOR WORLD DAY OF
PEACE, 2001

The breath of the divine life, the Holy Spirit, in its simplest and most common manner, expresses itself and makes itself felt in prayer. It is a beautiful and salutary thought that, wherever people are praying in the world, there the Holy Spirit is, the living breath of prayer.

DOMINUM ET VIVIFICANTEM, 1986

The Spirit instills in us a desire for the world to come, but he also inspires, purifies, and strengthens those noble longings by which we strive to make earthly life more human.

HOMILY AT AQUEDUCT RACETRACK,
NEW YORK, 1995

We can think of the Holy Spirit as the soul of our soul, and thus the secret of our sanctification. Let us dwell in his powerful and discreet, intimate and transforming presence!

GENERAL AUDIENCE, ROME, 1998

Love

When a person is entirely open to the breath of God's love, he becomes caught up in a spiritual "adventure" far beyond anything imaginable.

HOMILY, ROME, 1993

———

Love can overcome great obstacles, and God's love can totally transform the world.

MEETING WITH CHARITIES,
SAN ANTONIO, 1987

———

Authentic love is not a vague sentiment or a blind passion. It is an inner attitude that involves the whole human being. It is looking at others, not to use them but to serve them. It is the ability to rejoice with those who are rejoicing and to suffer with those who are suffering. It is sharing what one possesses so that no one may continue to be deprived of what he needs. Love, in a word, is the gift of self.

ANGELUS PRAYER, ROME, 1994

The vocation to love, understood as true openness to our fellow human beings and solidarity with them, is the most basic of all vocations. It is the origin of all vocations in life.

HOMILY FOR 1995 WORLD YOUTH
DAY'S PRAYER VIGIL, PHILIPPINES

Man cannot live without love. He remains a being that is incomprehensible for himself, his life is senseless, if love is not revealed to him, if he does not encounter love, if he does not experience it and make it his own, if he does not participate intimately in it.

REDEMPTOR HOMINIS, 1979

Christ is the King of love and therefore the final judgment on man and his world will be a judgment on love. Our place on one side or the other will depend on whether or not we have loved. The kingdom Christ offers us is also a task given to each of us. It is our responsibility to bring it about through those acts of love described with great realism by the Gospel.

HOMILY FOR THE FEAST OF
CHRIST THE KING, ROME, 1996

Real love is demanding. I would fail in my mission if I did not clearly tell you so. For it was Jesus—our Jesus Himself—who said, "You are my friends if you do what I command you" (John 15:14). Love demands effort and a personal commitment to the will of God. It means discipline and sacrifice, but it also means joy and human fulfillment.

SPEECH, BOSTON, 1979

Love and life according to the gospel cannot be thought of first and foremost as a kind of precept, because what they demand is beyond man's abilities. They are possible only as the result of a gift of God who heals, restores, and transforms the human heart by his grace. . . .

VERITATIS SPLENDOR, 1993

The central value, upon which other values in love depend, is the value of the human person. It is to the human person that basic responsibility refers. The texts of the Second Vatican Council affirm many times that love in general, and conjugal love in particular, consists in the gift of one person to another, a gift that embraces the human being as a whole, soul and body.

FRUITFUL AND RESPONSIBLE LOVE, 1979

The message of love that Christ brought is always important, always relevant. It is not difficult to see how today's world, despite its beauty and grandeur, despite the conquests of science and technology, despite the refined and abundant material good that it offers, is yearning for more truth, for more love, for more joy. And all of this is found in Christ and His way of life.

SPEECH, BOSTON, 1979

To imitate and live out the love of Christ is not possible for man by his own strength alone. He becomes capable of this love only by virtue of a gift received. As the Lord Jesus receives the love of his Father, so he in turn freely communicates that love to his disciples: "As the Father has loved me, so have I loved you. Live on in my love" (John 15:9).

VERITATIS SPLENDOR, 1993

Social Justice

Men are thirsty for love, for brotherly charity, but there are also whole peoples who are thirsty for the water necessary for their life.

ADDRESS, UPPER VOLTA, AFRICA, 1980

No one can consider himself extraneous or indifferent to the lot of another member of the human family. No one can say that he is not responsible for the well-being of his brother or sister.

CENTESIMUS ANNUS, 1991

We cannot stand idly by when thousands of human beings are dying of hunger. Nor can we remain indifferent when the rights of the human spirit are trampled upon.

ADDRESS TO 50TH SESSION OF THE
UNITED NATIONS, 1995

We must see another's poverty as our own and be convinced that the poor can wait no longer.

> HOMILY, SANTO DOMINGO,
> DOMINICAN REPUBLIC, 1992

We must all work for a world in which no child will be deprived of peace and security, of a stable family life, of the right to grow up without fear and anxiety.

> ADDRESS AT DEPARTURE CEREMONIES,
> ABUJA, NIGERIA, 1998

Do everything in order that there may disappear, at least gradually, that abyss which separates the excessively rich, few in number, from the great crowds of the poor, of those who live in want. Do everything so that this abyss may not increase but be reduced, that social equality may be aimed at, that the unjust distribution of goods may make way for a more just distribution.

> ADDRESS, SAO PÁULO, BRAZIL, 1980

Solutions must be sought on the global level by establishing a true economy of communion and sharing of goods, in both the national and international order.

ADDRESS, SANTO DOMINGO,
DOMINICAN REPUBLIC, 1992

Social justice cannot be attained by violence. Violence kills what it intends to create.

ADDRESS TO WORKERS IN SAO PÁULO,
BRAZIL, 1980

The distinctive mark of the Christian, today more than ever, must be love for the poor, the weak, the suffering. Living out this demanding commitment requires a total reversal of the alleged values which make people seek only their own good: power, pleasure, the unscrupulous accumulation of wealth. Yes, it is precisely to this radical conversion that Christ's disciples are called.

MESSAGE FOR WORLD DAY OF PEACE,
1998

Commitment to the poor is based on the Gospel: it does not have to rely on some political manifesto.

> SPEECH AT THE THIRD CONFERENCE
> OF LATIN AMERICAN BISHOPS, PUEBLA,
> MEXICO, 1979

The splendor of Christ's glory is reflected in the face of every human being, and is even more so when that face is emaciated by hunger, saddened by exile, or oppressed by poverty and misery.

> MESSAGE TO CATHOLIC RELIEF
> SERVICES, 1995

The poor of the United States and of the world are your brothers and sisters in Christ. You must never be content to leave them just the crumbs from the feast. You must take of your substance, and not just of your abundance, in order to help them. And you must treat them like guests at your family table.

> HOMILY, YANKEE STADIUM, NEW
> YORK, 1979

Family Life

When a man and a woman are united by true love, each one takes on the destiny, the future of the other, as his or her own.

AN INVITATION TO JOY

Marriage and the family are very deeply connected with man's personal dignity. They are not derived only from instinct and passion, nor only from feeling; they are derived in the first place from a decision of the free will, from a personal love, because of which spouses become not only one flesh, but also one heart and soul.

ADDRESS, COLOGNE, GERMANY, 1980

The family is the first school of living, and the influence received inside the family is decisive for the future development of the individual.

MESSAGE FOR WORLD DAY OF PEACE, 1998

The family is the sanctuary of life.

CENTESIMUS ANNUS, 1991

The family is the basic cell of society. It is the cradle of life and love, the place in which the individual "is born" and "grows."

CHRISTIFIDELES LAICI, 1988

The deepest human problems are connected with the family. It constitutes the primary, fundamental and irreplaceable community for man.

GENERAL AUDIENCE, ROME, 1978

The bond that unites a family is not only a matter of natural kinship or of shared life and experience. It is essentially a holy and religious bond. Marriage and the family are sacred realities.

PASTORAL VISIT TO THE UNITED STATES, 1987

In affirming that the spouses, as parents, cooperate with God the Creator in conceiving and giving birth to a new human being, we are not speaking merely with reference to the laws of biology. Instead, we wish to emphasize that God *himself is present in human fatherhood and motherhood* quite differently than he is present in all other instances of begetting "on earth." Indeed, God alone is the source of that "image and likeness" which is proper to the human being, as it was received at Creation. Begetting is the continuation of creation.

FAMILIARIS CONSORTIO, 1981

The physical and at the same time spiritual nature of conjugal communion, always enlightened by personal love, must lead to respect for sexuality, its fully human dimension, and never to use it as an "object," in order not to dissolve the personal union of soul and body. . . . The responsibility for the generation of human life—the life which must be born in a family—is great before God!

ADDRESS, LISBON, PORTUGAL, 1982

Far from promising his married followers an earthly paradise, Jesus Christ offers them the opportunity and the vocation to make a journey with him which, through difficulties and suffering, will strengthen their union and lead them to a greater joy, as proven by the experience of so many Christian couples, in our day as well.

GENERAL AUDIENCE, ROME, 1994

Inspired and sustained by the new commandment of love, the Christian family welcomes, respects and serves every human being, considering each one in his or her dignity as a person and as a child of God.

FAMILIARIS CONSORTIO, 1981

Responsible parenthood is the necessary condition for human love, and it is also the necessary condition for authentic conjugal love, because love cannot be irresponsible. Its beauty is the fruit of responsibility. When love is truly responsible, it is also truly free.

CROSSING THE THRESHOLD OF HOPE

It is above all in *raising children* that the family fulfils its mission to proclaim the *Gospel of life*. By word and example, in the daily round of relations and choices, and through concrete actions and signs, parents lead their children to authentic freedom, actualized in the sincere gift of self, and they cultivate in them respect for others, a sense of justice, cordial openness, dialogue, generous service, solidarity and all the other values which help people to live life as a gift.

EVANGELIUM VITAE, 1995

It is above all in the home that, before ever a word is spoken, children should experience God's love in the love which surrounds them. In the family they learn that God wants peace and mutual understanding among all human beings, who are called to be one great family.

MESSAGE FOR WORLD DAY OF PEACE, 1996

The family celebrates the gospel of life through daily prayer, both individual prayer and family prayer. The family prays in order to glorify and give thanks to God for the gift of life, and implores his light and strength in order to face times of difficulty and suffering without losing hope. But the celebration that gives meaning to every other form of prayer and worship is found in the family's actual daily life together, if it is a life of love and self-giving.

EVANGELIUM VITAE, 1995

The domestic virtues, based upon a profound respect for human life and dignity, and practiced in understanding, patience, mutual encouragement and forgiveness, enable the community of the family to live out the first and fundamental experience of peace.

MESSAGE FOR WORLD DAY OF PEACE, 1994

In the family, which is a community of persons, special attention must be devoted to the children by developing a profound esteem for their personal dignity, and a great respect and generous concern for their rights. This is true for every child, but it becomes all the more urgent the smaller the child is and the more it is in need of everything when it is sick, suffering, or handicapped.

FAMILIARIS CONSORTIO, 1981

Society must strongly reaffirm the right of the child to grow up in a family in which, as far as possible, both parents are present. Fathers of families must accept their full share of responsibility for the lives and upbringing of their children. Both parents must spend time with their children and be personally interested in their moral and religious education. Children need not only material support from their parents, but more importantly a secure, affectionate, and morally correct family environment.

HOMILY AT AQUEDUCT RACETRACK,
NEW YORK, 1995

If at every stage of his life man desires to be his own person, to find love, during his youth he desires it even more strongly. The desire to be one's own person, however, must not be understood as a license to do anything, without exception. The young do not want that at all— they are willing to be corrected, they want to be told yes or no. *They need guides,* and they want them close at hand.

CROSSING THE THRESHOLD OF HOPE

Forming children's viewing habits will sometimes mean simply turning off the television sets: because there are better things to do, because consideration for other family members requires it, or because indiscriminate television viewing can be harmful. Parents who make regular, prolonged use of television as a kind of electronic baby-sitter surrender their role as the primary educators of their children. Such dependence on television can deprive family members of opportunities to interact with one another through conversation, shared activities and common prayer.

MESSAGE FOR WORLD
COMMUNICATIONS DAY, 1994

The rights of the child may be summarized in its right to be loved, and the community cannot pretend to defend, protect, and support the child's development, if its initiatives are not based on a renewed awareness of the duty to love the child.

ADDRESS, ROME, 1993

There are cultures which manifest a unique veneration and great love for the elderly: far from being outcasts from the family or merely tolerated as a useless burden, they continue to be present and to take an active and responsible part in family life, though having to respect the autonomy of the new family; above all they carry out the important mission of being a witness to the past and a source of wisdom for the young and for the future.

FAMILIARIS CONSORTIO, 1981

It is therefore important to preserve, or to re-establish where it has been lost, a sort of "covenant" between generations. In this way parents, in their later years, can receive from their children the acceptance and solidarity which they themselves gave to their children when they brought them into the world.

EVANGELIUM VITAE, 1995

I repeat to you, you are the hope of the Pope. Do not deny me the joy of seeing you walk along paths that lead you to be real followers of good, and friends of Christ. Do not deny me the joy of your sense of responsibility in studies, activities and amusements. You are called to be bearers of generosity and honesty, to fight against immorality, to prepare a more just, healthier and happier world.

SPEECH TO 100,000 FAMILIES IN
GUADALAJARA, MEXICO, 1979

Peace in the World

The traditional problems of poverty, hunger, and disease have not yet been eradicated from our world. . . . In addition, new sources of tension and anxiety have emerged. The existence of immense arsenals of weapons of mass destruction causes a grave and justified uneasiness in our minds. The inequality of development favors some and plunges others into inextricable dependence. In these conditions, peace is fragile and injustice abounds.

ADDRESS GIVEN AT RAJ GHAT, THE
MEMORIAL TO MAHATMA GANDHI,
INDIA, 1986

It was not understood that a society worthy of the person is not built by destroying the person, by repression and by discrimination. This lesson of the Second World War has not yet been learned completely and in all quarters. And yet it remains and must stand as a warning for the next millennium.

MESSAGE ON THE 50TH ANNIVERSARY
OF THE END OF WORLD WAR II, 1995

All citizens have a duty to play an active part, in a spirit of solidarity, in the building of society, in consolidating peace between communities, and in managing the common good in an honest way. In order to do this common work that should bring together all the members of the same nation, it is right that everyone, Christians and Muslims, while respecting different religious views, should place their skills at the service of the nation, at every level of society.

HOMILY AT CAIRO SPORT PALACE,
EGYPT, 2000

We need to promote a peace-loving culture, inspired by sentiments of tolerance and universal solidarity. This culture does not reject a healthy patriotism, but keeps it far from exacerbated nationalism and narrowness. It is able to form great and noble souls, who are well aware that the wounds produced by hatred are not healed with bitterness, but rather with the therapy of patience and the balm of forgiveness.

ADDRESS UPON ARRIVAL IN CROATIA,
1994

If it is to be true and lasting, peace must be truly *human*. The desire for peace is universal. It is embedded in the hearts of all human beings, and it cannot be achieved unless the human person is placed at the center of every effort to bring about unity and brotherhood among nations.

ADDRESS, WASHINGTON, D.C., 1979

Humanity should question itself, once more, about the absurd and always unfair phenomenon of war, on whose stage of death and pain only remain standing the negotiating table that could and should have prevented it.

ADDRESS ON ARRIVAL TO BUENOS AIRES, NEAR THE END OF THE FALKLAND ISLANDS CONFLICT, 1982

In the face of the man-made calamity that every war is, one must affirm and reaffirm, again and again, that the waging of war is not inevitable or unchangeable. Humanity is not destined to self-destruction. Clashes of ideologies, aspirations, and needs can and must be settled and resolved by means other than war and violence. Humanity owes it to itself to settle differences and conflicts by peaceful means.

ADDRESS AT THE PEACE MEMORIAL, HIROSHIMA, JAPAN, 1981

War is not inevitable; peace is possible! It is possible because man has a conscience and a heart. It is possible because God loves each one of us, just as each one is, so as to transform and make him or her grow.

ADDRESS, ROME, 1994

In the face of the instruments of destruction and death, in the face of violence and cruelty, we have no other recourse but to God, with our words and with our hearts. We are neither strong nor powerful, but we know that God does not leave unanswered the entreaty of those who turn to Him with sincere faith, especially when the present and future destiny of millions of people is at stake.

ADDRESS, ROME, 1993

We will not accept that war should dominate life, the world, and people's day-to-day existence.

INTERNATIONAL PRAYER FOR PEACE MEETING, AACHEN, GERMANY, 2003

Among the signs of hope we should also count the spread, at many levels of public opinion, of *a new sensitivity ever more opposed to war* as an instrument for the resolution of conflicts between peoples, and increasingly oriented to finding effective but "non-violent" means to counter the armed aggressor.

EVANGELIUM VITAE, 1995

The building of links among peoples means the rediscovery and reassertion of all the values that reinforce peace and that join people together in harmony. This also means the renewal of what is best in the heart of man, the heart that seeks the good of the other in friendship and love.

NEGOTIATION: THE ONLY REALISTIC
SOLUTION TO THE CONTINUING
THREAT OF WAR

At this time when in so many places the mounting, inhuman din of war is heard once again, our world needs believers who raise their voices forcefully to intercede for peace. The prayers offered during these days is joined to the cry of the oppressed and the desire of millions of men and women who want to live in peace and security.

PAPAL LETTER TO "PRAYER MEETING
FOR PEACE," 1992

Anyone who decides that the peaceful means provided by international law are exhausted saddles himself with a heavy responsibility to God, to his conscience, and to history.

POPE JOHN PAUL II'S WORDS ON
IMPENDING WAR IN IRAQ, MARCH 18,
2003

When war, as in these days in Iraq, threatens the fate of humanity, it is ever more urgent to proclaim, with a strong and decisive voice, that only peace is the road to follow to construct a more just and united society. Violence and arms can never resolve the problems of men.

ADDRESS FOLLOWING THE START OF
THE IRAQ WAR, MARCH 22, 2003

Speaking to Youth

I am privileged to be able to meet young people in different places; but I am not so young myself now. When I entered the building, I met the organizers of this meeting and I asked them: "Up until what age can a person be considered young?" They answered, "Up until age forty." I responded, "Then for me there is no hope." Nevertheless, I keep repeating my meetings, and to this very day I have never been rejected by youth!

MEETING WITH YOUTH, MALI, 1990

What is beautiful about you is that each of you looks at other children and offers a hand with no regard for color, social condition, or religion. You offer your hand to one another. . . . All children are important. All of them!

SPEECH TO YOUTH, SALVADOR, BRAZIL,
1991

You are worth what your heart is worth.

SPEECH TO YOUTH, FRANCE, 1980

There is always a special attraction in you young people, because of that instinctive goodness of yours not contaminated by evil, and because of your particular readiness to accept truth, and put it into practice. And since God is truth, you, loving and accepting truth, are nearest to heaven.

ADDRESS, ROME, 1978

When young people like you or older people like me take the time to meet one another and to show their friendship, simply and sincerely, to help one another as best they can, that is happiness on earth! . . .

SPEECH TO YOUTH, MONTREAL,
CANADA, 1984

I talk to you with all my heart because, following Jesus' example, I say to you once again: The Pope has a great love for children! I want to see you grow up happy.

SPEECH TO YOUTH, SALVADOR, BRAZIL,
1991

A special characteristic of the young people of our time is openness—openness to the great cultural diversity of our world. But you must also be open to Christ.

SPEECH TO YOUTH, SCANDINAVIA, 1989

Do not be afraid! Life with Christ is a wonderful adventure. He alone can give full meaning to life, he alone is the center of history. Live by him!

SPEECH TO YOUTH, CZECH REPUBLIC, 1997

The way Jesus shows you is not easy. Rather, it is like a path winding up a mountain. Do not lose heart! The steeper the road, the faster it rises toward ever wider horizons.

MESSAGE FOR WORLD YOUTH DAY, 1996

Prepare for life with seriousness and diligence. Always remember that only if one builds, as St. Paul says, on the one foundation which is Jesus Christ, will one be able to construct something really great and lasting. With the liveliness that is characteristic of your age, with the generous enthusiasm of your young hearts, walk towards Christ. He alone is the solution to all your problems. He alone is the way, the truth and the life; he alone is the real salvation of the world; he alone is the hope of mankind.

SPEECH TO YOUTH, GUADALAJARA, MEXICO, 1979

When you wonder about the mystery of yourself, look to Christ, who gives you the meaning of life. When you wonder what it means to be a mature person, look to Christ, who is the fulfillness of humanity. And when you wonder about your role in the future of the world . . . look to Christ.

SPEECH TO STUDENTS, NEW YORK CITY, 1979

Christ offers you his friendship. He gave his life so that those who wish to answer his call can indeed become his friends. His is a friendship which is deep, genuine, loyal, and total, as all true friendship must be.

SPEECH TO YOUTH, CUBA, 1998

Jesus offers a very different message. Not far from this very place Jesus called his first disciples, as he calls you now. His call has always demanded a choice between the two voices competing for your hearts even now on this hill, the choice between good and evil, between life and death. Which voice will the young people of the twenty-first century choose to follow? To put your faith in Jesus means choosing to believe what he says, no matter how strange it may seem, and choosing to reject the claims of evil, no matter how sensible or attractive they may seem.

HOMILY AT YOUTH MASS, KORAZIM,
MOUNT OF THE BEATITUDES, 2000

Cry out, young university students, by witnessing to your faith! Do not be satisfied with a mediocre life without spiritual enthusiasm that is bent only upon achieving your own immediate personal advantage.

ADDRESS TO UNIVERSITY STUDENTS,
ROME, 2001

God calls every person, and his voice makes itself heard even in the hearts of children: he calls people to live in marriage or to be priests; he calls them to the consecrated life or perhaps to work in the missions. . . . Who can say? Pray, dear boys and girls, that you will find out what your calling is, and that you will follow it generously.

LETTER OF THE POPE TO CHILDREN,
1994

Christ is knocking very hard at many hearts, looking for young people like you to send into the vineyard where an abundant harvest is ready.

ADDRESS ON WORLD YOUTH DAY,
DENVER, 1993

We all have our personal history and an innate desire to see God, a desire which makes itself felt at the same time as we discover the created world. This world is wonderful and rich; it sets before us countless treasures; it enchants us; it attracts both our reason and our will. But in the end it does not satisfy our spirit. Man realizes that this world, with all its many riches, is superficial and precarious; in a sense, it is destined for death.

MESSAGE FOR WORLD YOUTH DAY,
1997

Yes, dear young people, do not close your eyes to the moral sickness that stalks your society today, and from which your youth alone will not protect you. How many young people have already warped their consciences and have substituted the true joy of life with drugs, sex, alcohol, vandalism and the empty pursuit of mere material possessions.

SPEECH TO YOUTH, GALWAY, IRELAND, 1979

Never forget that blindly following the impulse of emotions often means becoming a slave to our passions.

SPEECH TO YOUTH, CUBA, 1998

A serious moral crisis affects the lives of many young people, leaving them adrift. They are often without hope and are conditioned to look only for instant gratification. Yet everywhere there are young men and women deeply concerned about the world around them. They are ready to give the best of themselves in service to others. They are particularly sensitive to life's transcendent meaning.

ARRIVAL SPEECH TO THE PRESIDENT OF THE UNITED STATES ON THE EIGHTH WORLD YOUTH DAY, 1993

If you follow Jesus' advice and pray to God constantly, then you will learn to pray well. God himself will teach you.

SPEECH TO YOUTH, NEW ORLEANS, 1987

What enormous power the prayer of children has! This becomes a model for grown-ups themselves: praying with simple and complete trust means praying as children pray.

LETTER OF THE POPE TO CHILDREN, 1994

You instinctively turn away from hatred and are attracted by love: for this reason the Pope is certain that you will not refuse his request, but that you will join in his prayer for peace in the world with the same enthusiasm with which you pray for peace and harmony in your own families.

LETTER OF THE POPE TO CHILDREN, 1994

See to it that your youth is not only a purely transitory moment in your lives, but realize it fully by remaining united to the word of God, which is always young.

LETTER TO YOUTH, 1984

The Church entrusts to young people the task of proclaiming to the world the joy which springs from having met Christ. Dear friends, allow yourselves to be drawn to Christ; accept his invitation and follow him. Go and preach the good news that redeems; do it with happiness in your hearts and become communicators of hope in a world which is often tempted to despair.

MESSAGE FOR 1993 WORLD YOUTH DAY

Do not be afraid of presenting Christ to someone who does not yet know him. Christ is the true answer, the most complete answer to all the questions which concern the human person and his destiny. Without Christ, the human person remains an unsolvable riddle. Therefore, have the courage to present Christ! Certainly, you must do this in a way which respects each person's freedom of conscience, but you must do it.

MESSAGE FOR 1992 WORLD DAY OF YOUTH

The future belongs to you; for you are the leaders of tomorrow. As you plan and prepare for the future, it is right that you should aspire to greatness, that you should wish to accomplish great things in your lives. May you never give up these desires, but remain always men and women of high principles and hopes.

SPEECH TO YOUTH, SAINT LUCIA, 1986

Let me repeat once again, especially to you: "Do not be afraid! Put out into the deep," and go to meet Jesus confidently, since in him you will be free and safe, even when the paths of life become steep and threatening. Trust in him. . . .

ADDRESS TO UNIVERSITY STUDENTS, ROME, 2001

Prayer, Faith, and Holiness

I simply pray for everyone every day. As soon as I meet people, I pray for them, and this helps me in all my relationships. . . . I always follow this principle: I welcome everyone as a person sent to me and entrusted to me by Christ.

RISE, LET US BE ON OUR WAY

Our true mother tongue is the praise of God, the language of heaven, our true home. . . . As we look at the century we are leaving behind, we see that human pride and sin have made it difficult for many people to speak their mother tongue. In order to be able to sing God's praises we must relearn the language of humility and trust, the language of moral integrity and of sincere commitment to all that is truly good in the sight of the Lord.

EVENING OF PRAYER, ST. LOUIS, 1999

What is prayer? It is commonly held to be a conversation. In a conversation there are always an "I" and a "thou" or "you." In this case the "Thou" is with a capital T. If at first the "I" seems to be the most important element in prayer, prayer teaches that the situation is actually different. *The "Thou" is more important, because our prayer begins with God.*

CROSSING THE THRESHOLD OF HOPE

Prayer is the place where, in a very simple way, the creative and fatherly remembrance of God is made manifest: not only man's remembrance of God, but also and especially God's remembrance of man.

FAMILIARIS CONSORTIO, 1981

Prayer is indispensable for persevering in pursuit of the good, indispensable for overcoming the trials life brings to man owing to his weakness. Prayer is strength for the weak and weakness for the strong!

SIGN OF CONTRADICTION

Through prayer God reveals Himself above all as Mercy—that is, Love that goes out to those who are suffering, Love that sustains, uplifts, and invites us to trust. The victory of good in the world is united organically with this truth. A person who prays professes such a truth and in a certain sense makes God, who is *merciful Love*, present in the world.

CROSSING THE THRESHOLD OF HOPE

All prayer is a meeting between the human will and the will of God; for this we are indebted to the Son's obedience to the Father: "Your will be done." And obedience does not mean only renunciation of one's own will; it means opening one's spiritual eyes and ears to the Love which is God himself, God who loved the world so much that for its sake he sacrificed his only-begotten Son.

SIGN OF CONTRADICTION

In prayer we express to God our feelings, our thoughts, our sentiments. We wish to love and to be loved, to be understood and to understand. Only God loves us perfectly, with an everlasting love. In prayer, we open our hearts and our minds to this God of love. And it is prayer that makes us one with the Lord. Through prayer we come to share more deeply in God's life and in his love.

SPEECH TO YOUTH, NEW ORLEANS, 1987

Through the prayer of Christ to which we give voice, our day is sanctified, our activities transformed, our actions made holy. We pray the same psalms that Jesus prayed and come into personal contact with Him—the person to whom all Scripture points, the goal to which all history is directed.

SPEECH AT ST. PATRICK'S CATHEDRAL,
NEW YORK CITY, 1979

To say "Our Father . . . deliver us from evil" is to struggle within and around ourselves against that which aims at destroying the faith: indifference, systematic doubt, skepticism, as if happiness and the grandeur of man consisted in his liberating himself from God.

ADDRESS TO YOUTH, BRUSSELS,
BELGIUM, 1985

The rosary is my favorite prayer. A marvelous prayer! Marvelous in its simplicity and in its depth. In the prayer we repeat many times the words that the Virgin Mary heard from the Archangel, and from her kinswoman Elizabeth.

ADDRESS, ROME, 1978

Prayer can truly change your life. For it turns your attention away from yourself and directs your mind and your heart toward the Lord. If we look only at ourselves, with our limitations and sins, we quickly give way to sadness and discouragement. But if we keep our eyes fixed on the Lord, then our hearts are filled with hope, our minds are washed in the light of truth, and we come to know the fullness of the Gospel with all its promise and life.

SPEECH TO YOUTH, NEW ORLEANS,
1987

Prayer joined to sacrifice constitutes the most powerful force in human history.

ADDRESS, ROME, 1994

Prayer invites us to examine our consciences with regard to all the problems that afflict humanity. It invites us to evaluate our responsibilities, personal and collective, before God's judgment and in the light of human solidarity. For this reason, prayer transforms the world.

ADDRESS TO AMERICAN BISHOPS, 1988

Christian sensibility depends on prayer. Prayer is the essential condition—even if not the only one—*for a correct reading of the "signs of the times."* Without prayer we are inevitably deceived on this delicate subject.

ADDRESS TO AMERICAN BISHOPS, 1988

If you really wish to follow Christ, if you want your love for him to grow and last, then you must be faithful to prayer. It is the key to the vitality of your life in Christ. Without prayer, your faith and love will die. If you are constant in daily prayer and in the Sunday celebration of Mass, your love for Jesus will increase. And your heart will know deep joy and peace, such as the world could never give.

SPEECH TO YOUTH, NEW ORLEANS,
1987

Because he is made by God and bears within himself an indelible imprint of God, man is naturally drawn to God. When he heeds the deepest yearnings of the heart, every man must make his own the words of truth expressed by Saint Augustine: "You have made us for yourself, O Lord, and our hearts are restless until they rest in you."

EVANGELIUM VITAE, 1995

We will certainly encounter trials. There is nothing extraordinary about this, it is part of the life of faith. At times our trials will be light, at times they will be very difficult, or even dramatic. In our trials we may feel alone, but God's grace, the grace of a victorious faith, will never abandon us. Therefore we can expect to triumph over every trial, even the hardest.

RISE, LET US BE ON OUR WAY

Without faith in God, there can be no hope, no lasting, authentic hope. To stop believing in God is to start down a path that can lead only to emptiness and despair.

MESSAGE TO YOUTH TELECONFERENCE, LOS ANGELES, 1987

Faith is a gift of God which reaches man through the message of absolute truth, but it is, at the same time, *the response of the person* who sincerely seeks an encounter with God.

HOMILY, BRAZIL 1991

In the very search for faith an implicit faith is already present, and therefore the necessary condition for salvation is already satisfied.

CROSSING THE THRESHOLD OF HOPE

In particular, the life of holiness which is resplendent in so many members of the people of God, humble and often unseen, constitutes the simplest and most attractive way to perceive at once the beauty of truth, the liberating force of God's love, and the value of unconditional fidelity to all the demands of the Lord's law, even in the most difficult situations.

VERITATIS SPLENDOR, 1993

True holiness does not mean a flight from the world; rather, it lies in the effort to incarnate the Gospel in everyday life, in the family, at school and at work, and in social and political involvement.

MESSAGE TO CATHOLIC CHARISMATICS, 1996

My dear friends, what is holiness if not the joyful experience of the love of God and the encounter with him in prayer? Being holy means living in profound communication with the God of joy, having a heart free from sin and from the sadness of the world.

ADDRESS, ROME, 1995

God calls everyone to holiness, but without forcing anyone's hand. God asks and waits for man's free acceptance. In the context of this universal call to holiness, Christ then chooses a specific task for each person and if he finds a response, he himself provides for bringing the work he has begun to completion, ensuring that the fruit remains.

HOMILY AT THE BEATIFICATION OF
FIVE BLESSEDS, ROME, 1997

Morality

Morality is a just measure of humanity. Man fulfills himself in it and through it when he does good. When he performs evil, he destroys the order of morality within himself as well as in the interpersonal and social aspect of his existence.

BEATIFICATION LITURGY, POLAND, 1991

In a culture which holds that no universally valid truths are possible, nothing is absolute. Therefore, in the end—they say—objective goodness and evil no longer really matter. Good comes to mean what is pleasing or useful at a particular moment. Evil means what contradicts our subjective wishes. Each person can build a private system of values.

SPEECH TO YOUTH, DENVER, 1993

A society or culture which wishes to survive cannot declare the spiritual dimension of the human person to be irrelevant to public life.

AD LIMINA ADDRESS TO U.S. BISHOPS, 1998

It becomes necessary, therefore, on the part of all to recover an awareness of the primacy of moral values, which are the values of the human person as such. The great task that has to be faced today for the renewal of society is that of recapturing the ultimate meaning of life and its fundamental values.

FAMILIARIS CONSORTIO, 1981

Nothing "from outside" makes man filthy, no "material" dirt makes man impure in the moral, that is, interior sense. No ablution, not even of a ritual nature, is capable in itself of producing moral purity. This has its exclusive source within man; it comes from the heart.

GENERAL AUDIENCE, ROME, 1980

Human acts are moral acts because they express and determine the goodness or evil of the individual who performs them. They do not produce a change merely in the state of affairs outside of man but, to the extent that they are deliberate choices, they give moral definition to the very person who performs them, determining his profound spiritual traits.

VERITATIS SPLENDOR, 1993

The Ten Commandments are not an arbitrary imposition of a tyrannical Lord. They were written in stone; but before that, they were written on the human heart as the universal moral law, valid in every time and place. Today, as always, the Ten Words of the Law provide the only true basis for the lives of individuals, societies, and nations. Today, as always, they are the only future of the human family.

HOMILY AT ST. CATHERINE'S
MONASTERY, MOUNT SINAI, 2000

The command "Thou shall not kill" must be binding on the conscience of humanity if the terrible tragedy and destiny of Cain is not to be repeated.

ADDRESS, DROGHEDA, IRELAND, 1979

To keep the Commandments is to be faithful to God, but it is also to be faithful to ourselves, to our true nature and our deepest aspirations.

HOMILY AT ST. CATHERINE'S
MONASTERY, MOUNT SINAI, 2000

In the wake of so much suffering, you have the right to live in peace. Those who are guilty of disturbing this peace have many human victims on their conscience. They must understand that killing innocent human beings cannot be allowed. God once said, "You shall not kill." No man, no human association, no mafia can change or trample on this most sacred right of God. . . . In the name of the crucified and risen Christ, of Christ who is the Way and the Truth and the Life, I say to those who are responsible for this: "Repent! God's judgment will come some day!"

SPONTANEOUS ADDRESS AT THE END OF
MASS, SICILY, 1993

Young people, do not give in to this widespread false morality. Do not stifle your conscience! Conscience is the most secret core and sanctuary of a person, where we are alone with God.

SPEECH TO YOUTH, DENVER, 1993

Hope, Truth, and Freedom

Hope is not empty optimism springing from a naive confidence that the future will necessarily be better than the past. Hope and trust are the premise of responsible activity and are nurtured in that inner sanctuary of conscience where "man is alone with God" and thus perceives that *he is not alone* amid the enigmas of existence, for he is surrounded by the love of the Creator.

ADDRESS TO 50TH SESSION OF UNITED NATIONS, 1995

We cannot live without hope. We have to have some purpose in life, some meaning to our existence. We have to aspire to something. Without hope, we begin to die.

MESSAGE TO YOUTH TELECONFERENCE, LOS ANGELES, 1987

The Word stands poised between hope and despair. Yes, the Word of God gives us great reasons for hope. It is ever new, so splendid is the Word of God. It baffles the human mind with its incredible message.

LIFT UP YOUR HEARTS

As Jesus said, only the truth will make you free (cf. Jn 8:32). And the truth is not the fruit of each individual's imagination. God gave you intelligence to know the truth, and your will to achieve what is morally good. He has given you the light of conscience to guide your moral decisions, to love good and avoid evil. Moral truth is objective, and a properly formed conscience can perceive it.

SPEECH TO YOUTH, DENVER, 1993

Man cannot be forced to accept the truth. He can be drawn toward the truth only by his own nature, that is, by his own freedom, which commits him to search sincerely for truth and, when he finds it, to adhere to it both in his convictions and in his behavior.

CROSSING THE THRESHOLD OF HOPE

Freedom is not the ability to do anything we want, whenever we want. Rather, freedom is the ability to live responsibly the truth of our relationship with God and with one another.

ADDRESS TO YOUTH, ST. LOUIS, 1999

A certain concept of freedom, which has widespread support in public opinion at present, diverts attention from ethical responsibilities. Appeal is made today to freedom alone. It is often said: what matters is to be free, released from all constraint or limitation, so as to operate according to private judgment, which in reality is often pure caprice. This much is clear: such liberalism can only be described as primitive. Its influence, however, is potentially devastating.

MEMORY AND IDENTITY

Freedom is not simply the absence of tyranny or oppression. Nor is freedom the license to do whatever we like. Freedom has an inner "logic" which distinguishes it and ennobles it: freedom is ordered to the truth, and is fulfilled in man's quest for truth and in man's living in the truth.

ADDRESS TO 50TH SESSION OF UNITED NATIONS, 1995

Freedom is given to man by the Creator as a gift and at the same time as a task. Through freedom, man is called to accept and to implement the truth regarding the good. In choosing and bringing about a genuine good in personal and family life, in the economic and political sphere, in national and international arenas, man brings about his own freedom in the truth.

MEMORY AND IDENTITY

It would be a great tragedy for the entire human family if the United States, which prides itself on its consecration to freedom, were to lose sight of the true meaning of the noble world. America: You cannot insist on the right to choose, without also insisting on *the duty to choose well, the duty to choose the truth!*

ADDRESS AT PRAYER VIGIL, SOUTH
CAROLINA, 1987

The Equality of Human Beings

Is it any wonder that the pope who grew up here, who came from the diocese that included the camp at Auschwitz, should have wholly devoted himself to man, to the dignity of man, to the threats to man and his inalienable rights that can be so easily trampled underfoot and eradicated by man?

ADDRESS AT AUSCHWITZ DURING JOHN
PAUL II'S FIRST VISIT AS POPE, 1979

Life is a gift from the Creator, to be spent in the service of one's brothers and sisters who, in the plan of salvation, can always draw benefit from it. It is, therefore, never licit to harm its course, from its beginning to its natural end. Rather it is to be accepted, respected and promoted with every means available, and defended from every threat.

ADDRESS TO AN INTERNATIONAL
CONGRESS ON CARE OF THE DYING,
1992

Life, especially human life, belongs only to God. For this reason, whoever attacks human life in some way attacks God Himself.

EVANGELIUM VITAE, 1995

But God created all men equal in dignity, though different with regard to gifts and to talents. Mankind is a whole where each one has his part to play; the worth of the various peoples and of the diverse cultures must be recognized. The world is, as it were, a living organism; each culture has something to receive from the others, and has something to give to them.

ADDRESS TO UNITED NATIONS OFFI-
CIALS IN NAIROBI, KENYA, 1985

I do not hesitate to proclaim before you and before the world that all human life—from the moment of conception and through all subsequent stages—is sacred, because human life is created in the image and likeness of God. Nothing surpasses the greatness or dignity of a human person. . . . Human life is precious because it is the gift of a God whose love is infinite; and when God gives life, it is forever.

HOMILY, WASHINGTON, D.C., 1979

Recognition of someone as a human being is never based on the awareness or experience we may have of him, but by the certitude that he has an infinite value from conception, which comes to him from his relationship with God. A human being has primacy over the ideas others have of him, and his existence is absolute and not relative.

ADDRESS TO INTERNATIONAL MEETING
ON THE WELL-BEING OF WOMEN, 1996

Every human person—no matter how vulnerable or helpless, no matter how young or how old, no matter how healthy, handicapped or sick, no matter how useful or productive for society—is a being of inestimable worth created in the image and likeness of God. This is the dignity of America, the reason she exists, the condition for her survival—yes, the ultimate test of her greatness: to respect every human person, especially the weakest and most defenseless ones, those as yet unborn.

ADDRESS AT DETROIT AIRPORT, 1987

And you, who are you? For me you are first of all human beings, endowed with the immense dignity that is a condition of being a person, each one of you with the unique, unrepeatable personal features that God has given you. You are persons who have been saved by the blood of the One whom I like to call the "Redeemer of man," as I did in the first letter I wrote to the entire Church and the world. You are children of God, known and loved by him. You are and will be from now on and forever my friends, my very dear friends.

ADDRESS GIVEN AT LEPROSARIUM OF
MARITUBA, BRAZIL, 1980

The disabled person is one of us and participates fully in the same humanity that we possess. It would be radically unworthy of man, and a denial of our common humanity, to admit to the life of the community, and thus admit to work, only those who are fully functional. To do so would be to practice a serious form of discrimination, that of the strong and healthy against the weak and sick.

LABOREM EXERCENS, 1981

For man, the right to life is the *fundamental right*. And yet, a part of contemporary culture has wanted to deny that right, turning it into an "uncomfortable" right, one that has to be defended. But there is no other right that so closely affects the very existence of the person! The right to life means the right to be born and then continue to live until one's natural end: "As long as I live, I have the right to live."

CROSSING THE THRESHOLD OF HOPE

Man is called to a fullness of life which far exceeds the dimensions of his earthly existence, because it consists in sharing the very life of God. The loftiness of this supernatural vocation reveals the greatness and the inestimable value of human life even in its temporal phase.

EVANGELIUM VITAE, 1995

The Catholic Church teaches that every human being is composed of body and soul. It is the union of the body and the immortal soul, with its intellect and free will, that defines each person, who is unique and an expression of God's love. Although everyone must die, the soul is destined to live forever, and our bodies will rise again as well. Because human beings were made in the image and likeness of God and are destined for eternity, every human life is of infinite value.

ADDRESS, JAPAN, 1981

Suffering and Death

I remember that at the beginning the sick intimidated me. I needed a lot of courage to stand before a sick person and enter, so to speak, into his physical and spiritual pain, not to betray discomfort, and to show at least a little loving compassion. Only later did I begin to grasp the profound meaning of the mystery of human suffering. In the weakness of the sick, I saw emerging even more clearly a new strength—the strength of mercy.

RISE, LET US BE ON OUR WAY

In order to perceive the true answer to the "why" of suffering, we must look to the revelation of divine love, the ultimate source of the meaning of everything that exists. Love is also the richest source of the meaning of suffering, which always remains a mystery: we are conscious of the insufficiency and inadequacy of our explanations. Christ causes us to enter into the mystery and to discover the "why" of suffering, as far as we are capable of grasping the sublimity of divine love.

SALVIFICI DOLORIS, 1984

Jesus Christ has taken the lead on the way of the cross. He has suffered first. He does not drive us toward suffering but shares it with us, wanting us to have life and to have it in abundance.

MEETING WITH THE SICK AND SUFFERING, 1998

By dying on the cross, Christ reveals to us the meaning of our suffering. In his Passion we find the encouragement and strength to avoid every temptation to bitterness and, through pain, to grow into a new life. *Suffering is an invitation to be like the Son by doing the will of the Father.* We are offered the opportunity to imitate Christ, who died to redeem mankind from sin. Thus the Father wished suffering to enrich the individual and the whole Church.

ADDRESS, UNITED KINGDOM, 1982

This is the meaning of suffering, which is truly supernatural, and at the same time, human. It is supernatural because it is rooted in the divine mystery of the Redemption of the world, and it is likewise deeply human because in it, the person discovers himself, his own humanity, his own dignity, his own mission.

SALVIFICI DOLORIS, 1984

Earthly suffering, when accepted in love, is like a bitter kernel containing the seed of new life, the treasure of divine glory to be given man in eternity. Although the sight of a world burdened with evil and misfortunes of every sort is often so wretched, nevertheless the hope of a better world of love and grace is hidden within it. It is hope that is nourished on Christ's promise. With this support, those who suffer united with him already experience in this life a joy that can seem humanly unexplainable.

ADDRESS, ROME, 1994

At the very moment when I fell in St. Peter's Square I had this vivid presentiment that I should be saved. This certainty never let me, even at the worst moments, after the first operation and during the virus infection.

BE NOT AFRAID!

Now I know better than ever before that *suffering* is one of those dimensions of life in which more than ever *the grace of redemption is grafted onto the human heart.* And if I wish that each and every one of you may regain your health and leave this hospital, then with equal warmth I hope that you may take away from there the profound graft of divine life, which the grace of suffering carries with it.

ADDRESS AT GEMELLI HOSPITAL DUR-
ING HIS RECOVERY FROM THE ASSASSI-
NATION ATTEMPT, 1981

I, too, have been assailed by suffering and have known the physical weakness that comes from disability and illness. . . . Dear Friends, no force or power exists that can separate you from God's love. Illness and suffering seem contradictory to what is important for man and what man desires. And yet no malady, no weakness, no infirmity can deprive you of your dignity as children of God, as brothers and sisters of Jesus Christ.

ADDRESS, UNITED KINGDOM, 1982

Brothers in Christ, who know all the bitterness of the way of the Cross, be assured that you are not alone. *The Church* is with you, with the sacrament of salvation, to sustain you on your difficult road. The Church receives a great deal from your suffering, if it is confronted in faith; the Church is beside you with the comfort of the active solidarity of its members, so that you will never lose hope.

ADDRESS AT THE INTERNATIONAL
CONGRESS ON AIDS, 1989

God is on the side of the oppressed. He is beside the parents who cry for their murdered children; He hears the impotent cry of the defenseless and downtrodden; He is in solidarity with women humiliatingly violated; He is near to refugees forced to leave their land and their homes. Do not forget the sufferings of families, of the elderly, widows, the young and children. It is His people who are dying.

HOMILY AT THE MASS FOR SARAJEVO
AT CASTEL GANDOLFO, 1994

The Pope bows with devotion before old age, and he invites all people to do the same with him. Old age is the crown of the steps of life. It gathers in the harvest, the harvest from what you have learned and experienced, the harvest from what you have done and achieved, the harvest from what you have suffered and undergone. As in the finale of a great symphony, all the great themes of life combine to a mighty harmony.

ADDRESS, MUNICH, 1980

To forego extraordinary or disproportionate means is not the equivalent of suicide or euthanasia; it rather expresses acceptance of the human condition in the face of death.

EVANGELIUM VITAE, 1995

Our modern secularized societies run the risk of driving suffering, dying, and death out of their personal experience.

ADDRESS, ROME, 1992

The certainty that life continues in a different way from what our eyes behold brings believers to cemeteries. To stand at the graves of one's own loved ones is an occasion for families to reflect on and to nurture their hope in eternity.

GENERAL AUDIENCE FOR ALL SOULS
DAY, ROME, 1994

However, he [man] also experiences the irrepressible desire for immortal life. For this reason the bonds of love uniting parents and children, husbands and wives, brothers and sisters, as well as the ties of true friendship between individuals, are not lost nor do they end with the inescapable event of death. Our departed ones continue to live among us, not only because their mortal remains rest in the cemetery and their memory is part of our lives, but especially because their souls intercede for us with God.

GENERAL AUDIENCE FOR ALL SOULS
DAY, ROME, 1994

Before Christ I renew my vow to serve the Church as long as He wishes, giving myself up completely to His Holy Will. I leave the decision on how He will free me from this service entirely up to him.

POPE JOHN PAUL II, 1998

Death itself is anything but an event without hope. It is the door which opens wide on eternity and, for those who live in Christ, an experience of participation in the mystery of his Death and Resurrection.

EVANGELIUM VITAE, 1995

Sin and Forgiveness

The greatest obstacle to man's journey toward God is sin, perseverance in sin and, finally, denial of God—the deliberate blotting out of God from the world of human thought, the detachment from Him of the whole of man's earthly activity, the rejection of God by man.

HOMILY AT MASS IN FATIMA, 1982

As a rupture with God, sin is an act of disobedience by a creature who rejects, at least implicitly, the very one from whom he came and who sustains him in life. It is therefore a suicidal act. Since by sinning man refuses to submit to God, his internal balance is also destroyed and it is precisely within himself that contradictions and conflicts arise. Wounded in this way, man almost inevitably causes damage to the fabric of his relationship with others and with the created world.

RECONCILIATIO ET PAENITENTIA, 1984

Sin never occurs as something hidden and unexpected; it develops bit by bit. It may appear that it develops without our being aware of it; however, this is only an impression. It is not an unexpected thing, which takes us by surprise. The groundwork for it is laid in a certain way from outside—and, we must point out, from inside too.

THE WAY TO CHRIST

Sin, in the proper sense, is always a personal act, since it is an act of freedom on the part of an individual person, and not properly of a group or community. This individual may be conditioned, incited and influenced by numerous and powerful external factors. He may also be subjected to tendencies, defects and habits linked with his personal condition. In not a few cases such external and internal factors may attenuate, to a greater or lesser degree, the person's freedom and therefore his responsibility and guilt.

RECONCILIATIO ET PAENITENTIA, 1984

The mystery of sin is composed of this twofold wound which the sinner opens in himself and in his relationship with his neighbor. Therefore one can speak of personal and social sin: From one point of view, every sin is personal; from another point of view, every sin is social insofar as and because it also has social repercussions.

RECONCILIATIO ET PAENITENTIA, 1984

We must be radical with sin. If we do not strike with the ax at the root of selfishness, it will surface again and again. We cannot make progress in the ways of God without making this decision. The way has been so dramatically laid out for us in Jesus' temptations in the desert. We see him reject the deception of selfish ambition and pride to fully obey his divine call. By renouncing all ambition, he perfectly fulfilled the word of God and submitted to the Father's will.

LIFT UP YOUR HEARTS

Despite all the powerful forces of poverty and oppression, of evil and sin in all their forms, the power of truth will prevail—the truth about God, *the truth about man.*

ADDRESS, DELHI, INDIA, 1986

No human sin can erase the mercy of God or prevent him from unleashing all his triumphant power, if we only call upon him. Indeed, sin itself makes even more radiant the love of the Father. In order to ransom a slave, he sacrificed his Son: his mercy toward us is redemption.

VERITATIS SPLENDOR, 1993

Spirit of God, pour your light and your love into human hearts to achieve reconciliation between individuals, within families, between neighbors, in cities and villages, and within the institutions of civil society!

HOMILY AT THE NAVAL BASE
ESPLANADE, LEBANON, 1997

Forgiveness demonstrates the presence in the world of the love which is more powerful than sin. Forgiveness is also the fundamental condition for reconciliation, not only in the relationship of God with man, but also in relationships between people.

DIVES IN MISERICORDIA, 1980

Forgiving one's enemies, as the martyrs of all ages have done, is the decisive truth and authentic expression of the radical nature of Christian love.

ADDRESS, EL SALVADOR, 1996

"Forgiveness" is a word spoken by the lips of a man to whom some evil has been done. It is, in fact, the word of the human heart. In this word of the heart each of us endeavors to go beyond the frontier of hostility, which can separate us from the other; he tries to reconstruct the interior space of understanding, contact, bond.

ADDRESS, ROME, 1981

What we talked about will have to remain a secret between him and me. I spoke to him as a brother whom I have pardoned and who has my complete trust.

ON VISITING THE IMPRISONED
MEHMET ALI AGCA, WHO WOUNDED
THE POPE IN A 1981 ASSASSINATION
ATTEMPT, AS REPORTED IN TIME,
JANUARY, 1984

Throughout His life, Jesus proclaimed God's forgiveness, but He also taught the need for mutual forgiveness as the condition for obtaining it. In the Lord's Prayer, He makes us pray: "Forgive us our trespasses, as we forgive those who trespass against us." With that *as*, He places in our hands the measure with which we shall be judged by God.

MESSAGE FOR WORLD DAY OF PEACE,
1997

Confession is an act of honesty and courage; an act of entrusting our-selves, beyond sin, to the mercy of a loving and forgiving God. It is an act of the prodigal son who returns to his Father and is welcomed by him with the kiss of peace.

HOMILY, SAN ANTONIO, 1987

To accept and give forgiveness makes possible a new quality of rap-port between men, interrupting the spiral of hatred and revenge and breaks the chains of evil which bind the heart of rivals. For nations in search of reconciliation and for those hoping for peaceful coexis-tence among individuals and peoples, there is no other way than for-giveness received and offered.

MESSAGE FOR LENT, 2001

The Church

The Church has endured for 2000 years. Like the *mustard seed* in the Gospel, she has grown and become a great tree, able to cover the whole of humanity with her branches.

TERTIO MILLENNIO ADVENIENTE, 1994

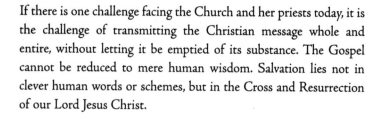

If there is one challenge facing the Church and her priests today, it is the challenge of transmitting the Christian message whole and entire, without letting it be emptied of its substance. The Gospel cannot be reduced to mere human wisdom. Salvation lies not in clever human words or schemes, but in the Cross and Resurrection of our Lord Jesus Christ.

ADDRESS AT ST. JOSEPH'S SEMINARY,
NEW YORK, 1995

Following Christ, the Church seeks the truth, which is not always the same as the majority opinion. She listens to conscience and not to power, and in this way she defends the poor and the downtrodden.

FAMILIARIS CONSORTIO, 1981

See [The Church] cannot cross the threshold of the new millennium without encouraging her children to purify themselves, through repentance, of past errors and instances of infidelity, inconsistency, and slowness to act. Acknowledging the weaknesses of the past is an act of honesty and courage which helps us to strengthen our faith.

TERTIO MILLENNIO ADVENIENTE, 1994

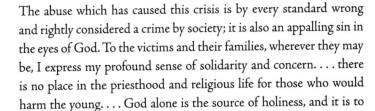

The abuse which has caused this crisis is by every standard wrong and rightly considered a crime by society; it is also an appalling sin in the eyes of God. To the victims and their families, wherever they may be, I express my profound sense of solidarity and concern. . . . there is no place in the priesthood and religious life for those who would harm the young. . . . God alone is the source of holiness, and it is to him above all that we must turn for forgiveness, for healing and for the grace to meet this challenge with uncompromising courage and harmony of purpose.

ADDRESS OF POPE JOHN PAUL II TO CARDINALS OF THE U.S., APRIL 23, 2002

Admittedly, the Church, as a human institution, is continually in need of purification and renewal: the Second Vatican Council acknowledged this with courageous candor. Yet the Church, as the Body of Christ, is the normal locus for the presence and action of Christ in the world.

MEMORY AND IDENTITY

In God's plan, the Church is not a means to be used for some common enterprise, no matter how noble and useful, Rather, the Church as she comes to us from the loving hand of the Father is the sign and the instrument of the human family's communion with God himself and of its own deepest unity.

ADDRESS TO THE SPECIAL ASSEMBLY OF AFRICAN BISHOPS, KENYA, 1995

The aim of any service in the Church, whether the service is apostolic, pastoral, priestly, or episcopal, is to keep up this dynamic link between the mystery of the Redemption and every man.

REDEMPTOR HOMINIS, 1979

In the Church there are many different gifts. There is room for many different cultures and ways of doing things. But there is no room in the Church for selfishness.

SPEECH TO YOUTH, NEW ORLEANS,
1987

The mission of the Church in the world is accomplished not only by ministers who have received the sacraments of orders, but also by all the lay faithful. Because they have been baptized, the lay faithful share in the priestly, prophetic and royal functions of Christ.

ADDRESS, RÉUNION, 1989

The Church must constantly look for new ways that will enable her to understand more profoundly and to carry out with renewed vigor the mission received from her Founder.

ADDRESS, IRELAND, 1979

The Blessed Mother

Mary is the new Eve, placed by God in close relation to Christ, the new Adam, beginning with the Annunciation, through the night of His birth in Bethlehem, through the wedding feast at Cana of Galilee, through the Cross at Calvary, and up to the gift of the Holy Spirit at Pentecost. The Mother of Christ the Redeemer is the Mother of the Church.

CROSSING THE THRESHOLD OF HOPE

I entrust this responsibility of the whole Church to the maternal intercession of Mary, Mother of the Redeemer. She, the mother of fairest love, will be for Christians on the way to the Great Jubilee of the third millennium the star which safely guides their steps to the Lord.

TERTIO MILLENNIO ADVENIENTE, 1994

Mary shares our human condition, but in complete openness to the grace of God. Not having known sin, she is able to have compassion for every kind of weakness. She understands sinful man and loves with a mother's love.

VERITATIS SPLENDOR, 1993

The Blessed Virgin Mary, the first of the redeemed, the first to have been closely associated with the work of Redemption, will always be your guide and model.

ADDRESS, ROME, 1983

In the light of Mary, the Church sees in the face of women the reflection of a beauty which mirrors the loftiest sentiments of which the human heart is capable: the self-offering totality of love; the strength that is capable of bearing the greatest sorrows; limitless fidelity and tireless devotion to work; the ability to combine penetrating intuition with words of support and encouragement.

REDEMPTORIS MATER, 1987

Mary's motherhood, which becomes man's inheritance, is a gift: a gift which Christ himself makes personally to every individual.

REDEMPTORIS MATER, 1987

Motherhood means caring for the life of the child. Since Mary is the mother of us all, her care for the life of man is universal. The care of a mother embraces her child totally. Mary's motherhood has its beginning in her motherly care for Christ. In Christ, at the foot of the cross, she accepted John, and in John she accepted all of us totally.

HOMILY AT MASS IN FATIMA, 1982

This woman of faith, Mary of Nazareth, the Mother of God, has been given to us as a model in our pilgrimage of faith. From Mary we learn to surrender to God's will in all things. From Mary, we learn to trust even when all hope seems gone. From Mary, we learn to love Christ, her Son and the Son of God. For Mary is not only the Mother of God, she is Mother of the Church as well.

MESSAGE TO PRIESTS, WASHINGTON D.C., 1979

Like Mary, you must not be afraid to allow the Holy Spirit to help you become intimate friends of Christ. Like Mary, you must put aside any fear, in order to take Christ to the world in whatever you do—in marriage, as single people in the world, as students, as workers, as professional people. Christ wants to go to many places in the world, and to enter many hearts, through you.

HOMILY AT CENTRAL PARK, NEW YORK, 1995

She is the woman of glory in whom God's plan could be carried out with supreme perfection.

EVANGELIUM VITAE, 1995

Was it not for our encouragement that God chose to come to us through the Immaculate Virgin, conceived without sin? From the first moment of her existence she was never under the power of sin, while we are called to be cleansed of sin by opening our heart to the merciful Redeemer whom she brought into this world. There is no better way to approach her Son than through her.

ADDRESS, NAGASAKI, JAPAN, 1981

Priests

The priestly vocation is a mystery. *It is the mystery of a "wondrous exchange"—admirabile commercium—*between God and man. A man offers his humanity to Christ, so that Christ may use him as an instrument of salvation, making him as it were into another Christ. Unless we grasp the mystery of this "exchange," we will not understand how it can be that a young man, hearing the words "Follow me!," can give up everything for Christ, in the certainty that if he follows this path he will find complete personal fulfillment.

GIFT AND MYSTERY

If we take a close look at what contemporary men and women expect from priests, we will see that, in the end, they have but one great expectation: *they are thirsting for Christ.* Everything else—their economic, social, and political needs—can be met by any number of other people. From the priest they ask for Christ!

GIFT AND MYSTERY

Dear Brothers in the priesthood, let us never tire of being witnesses and heralds of Christ, let us never be discouraged by the difficulties and obstacles we find either within us, in our human frailty, or in the indifference or lack of understanding of those to whom we are sent, including sometimes the persons who are close to us. Whenever difficulties and temptations weigh on our hearts, let us very much remember *the greatness of the gift we have received to be able in our turn to "give with joy"* (cf. 2 Cor. 9:7).

ADDRESS TO THE PRIESTS OF ROME, 2003

Before being organizers of your communities, be models of prayer and spiritual perfection for them. By constant recourse to prayer you will be able to draw on the inner strength necessary to overcome difficulties, conquer temptations, and grow in charity and fidelity to your vocation.

ADDRESS, SORRENTO, 1992

It is in the confessional that every priest becomes a witness of the great miracles which divine mercy works in souls which receive the grace of conversion. It is necessary, however, that every priest at the service of his brothers and sisters in the confessional should experience this same divine mercy by going regularly to confession himself and by receiving spiritual direction.

GIFT AND MYSTERY

The priest who, in the choice of celibacy, renounces human love to be opened totally to that of God, makes himself free to be given to men by a gift excluding no one, but including them all in the flow of charity which comes from God (cf. Rom 5:5) and leads to God. Celibacy, in linking the priest to God, frees him for all the works required by the care of souls.

ADDRESS TO PRIESTS, ZAIRE, 1980

Some, seeking to argue against the discipline of celibacy, draw attention to the loneliness of a priest or a bishop. On the basis of my own experience, I firmly reject this argument. Personally, I have never felt lonely. Aside from constant awareness that the Lord is close at hand, I have always been surrounded by people, and I have maintained cordial relations with priests—deans, pastors, assistant pastors—and with all kinds of lay people.

RISE, LET US BE ON OUR WAY

No priest can carry out his ministry well unless he lives in union with Christ. His life, like Christ's, must be marked by self-sacrifice, zeal for the spreading of the Kingdom of God, unblemished chastity, unstinted charity. All this is possible only when the priest is a man of prayer and Eucharistic devotion. . . . In silent prayer before the Blessed Sacrament, he will be constantly renewed in his consecration to Jesus Christ and confirmed in his permanent commitment to priestly celibacy.

ADDRESS TO SEMINARIANS, NIGERIA, 1982

If Christ—by his free and sovereign choice, clearly attested to by the Gospel and by the Church's constant Tradition—entrusted only to men the task of being an "icon" of his countenance as "shepherd" and "bridegroom" of the Church through the exercise of the ministerial priesthood, this in no way detracts from the role of women, or for that matter from the role of the other members of the Church who are not ordained to the sacred ministry, since *all* share equally in the dignity proper to the "common priesthood" based on Baptism.

LETTER TO WOMEN, 1995

In calling men only as his Apostles, Christ acted in a completely free and sovereign matter. In doing so, he exercised the same freedom with which, in all his behavior, he emphasized the dignity and the vocation of women, without conforming to the prevailing customs and to the traditions sanctioned by the legislation of the time.

MULIERIS DIGNITATEM, 1988

In considering our priests, we must not overlook those who have left the active ministry. The bishop cannot forget them. They too have a right to his paternal concern. Their stories sometimes indicate failures in priestly formation, which has to include courageous fraternal correction when it is called for. A priest, for his part, has to be ready to accept such correction. Christ said to his disciples: *"If your brother sins against you, go and tell him his fault between you and him alone. If he listens to you, you have won over your brother"* (Matt. 18:15).

RISE, LET US BE ON OUR WAY

Christ needs holy priests! Today's world demands holy priests! Only a holy priest can become, in an increasingly secularized world, a resounding witness to Christ and his Gospel. And only thus can a priest become a guide for men and women and a teacher of holiness. People, especially the young, are looking for such guides. A priest can be a guide and teacher only to the extent that he becomes an authentic witness!

GIFT AND MYSTERY

Women

In creating the human race "male and female," God gives man and woman an equal personal dignity, endowing them with the inalienable rights and responsibilities proper to the human person.

FAMILIARIS CONSORTIO, 1981

The Church would like to thank the Most Holy Trinity for the "mystery of woman," and, for every woman—for what constitutes the eternal measure of her feminine dignity, for the "great works of "God" which throughout human history have been accomplished in her and through her. After all, wasn't the greatest event in human history—the incarnation of God himself—accomplished in her and through her?

MULIERIS DIGNITATEM, 1988

History is written almost exclusively as the narrative of men's achievements, when in fact its better part is most often molded by women's determined and persevering action for good.

PAPAL MESSAGE ON WOMEN'S
CONFERENCE, 1995

Jesus always showed the greatest esteem and the greatest respect for woman, for every woman, and in particular he was sensitive to female suffering. Going beyond the religious and social barriers of the time, Jesus reestablished woman in her full dignity as a human person before God and before men.

ADDRESS, ROME, 1979

The work of building peace can hardly overlook the need to acknowledge and promote the dignity of women as persons, called to play a unique role in educating for peace.

ADDRESS, ROME, 1994

In order to be a teacher of peace, a woman must first of all nurture peace within herself. Inner peace comes from knowing that one is loved by God and from the desire to respond to His love. History is filled with marvelous examples of women who, sustained by this knowledge, have been able successfully to deal with difficult situations of exploitation, discrimination, violence and war.

MESSAGE FOR 28TH WORLD DAY OF PEACE, 1995

In fact it is one thing to be conscious that the value of sex is a part of all the rich storehouse of values with which the female appears to the male; it is another to "reduce" all the personal riches of femininity to that single value, that is, as a suitable object of gratification of sexuality itself. The same reasoning can be valid concerning what masculinity is for the woman.

GENERAL AUDIENCE, ROME 1980

The true advancement of women requires that labor should be structured in such a way that women do not have to pay for their advancement by abandoning what is specific to them and at the expense of the family, in which women as mothers have an irreplaceable role.

LABOREM EXERCENS, 1981

A mother's presence in the family, so critical to the stability and growth of that basic unity of society, should instead be recognized, applauded and supported in every possible way. By the same token society needs to *call husbands and fathers to their family responsibilities,* and ought to strive for a situation in which they will not be forced by economic circumstances to move away from the home in search of work.

PAPAL MESSAGE ON WOMEN'S
CONFERENCE, 1995

As most women themselves point out, *equality of dignity* does not mean "sameness with men." This would only impoverish women and all of society, by deforming or losing the unique richness and the inherent value of femininity.

PAPAL MESSAGE ON WOMEN'S
CONFERENCE, 1995

When women are able fully to share their gifts with the whole community, the very way in which society understands and organizes itself is improved and comes to reflect in a better way the substantial unity of the human family. Here we see the most important condition for the consolidation of authentic peace. The growing presence of women in social, economic and political life at the local, national and international levels is thus a very positive development.

WOMEN: TEACHERS OF PEACE, 1995

World Religions

Whenever violence is done in the name of religion, we must make it clear to everyone that in such instances we are not dealing with true religion.

ADDRESS TO MUSLIMS, ABUJA,
NIGERIA, 1998

To do harm, to promote violence and conflict in the name of religion, is a terrible contradiction and a great offense against God. But past and present history gives us many examples of such a misuse of religion. We must all work to strengthen the growing commitment to interreligious dialogue, a great sign of hope for the peoples of the world.

ADDRESS UPON ARRIVAL IN EGYPT,
2000

Religious tolerance is based on the conviction that God wishes to be adored by people who are free: a conviction which requires us to respect and honor the inner sanctuary of conscience in which each person meets God.

GREETING IN BALTIMORE CATHEDRAL,
MARYLAND, 1995

As for non-Christian religions, the Catholic Church rejects nothing in them which is true and holy. Hence, with regard to other religions Catholics intend to emphasize elements of truth wherever they are to be found, while at the same time firmly bearing witness to the newness of the revelation of Christ, preserved in its fullness by the Church. Consistent with this attitude, they reject as alien to the spirit of Christ any discrimination or persecution directed against persons on the basis of race, color, condition of life or religion. Difference of religion must never be a cause of violence or war. Instead persons of different beliefs must feel themselves drawn, precisely because of these beliefs, to work together for peace and justice.

ECCLESIA IN AMERICA, 1999

Abraham, our common ancestor, teaches all of us, Christians, Jews and Muslims, to follow this way of mercy and love.

ADDRESS, LISBON, PORTUGAL, 1982

Personally, I have always wanted to be counted among those who work, on both sides, to overcome old prejudices and to secure ever wider and fuller recognition of the spiritual patrimony shared by Jews and Christians. . . . We hope that the Jewish people will acknowledge that the Church utterly condemns anti-Semitism and every form of racism as being altogether opposed to the principles of Christianity.

VISIT TO TWO CHIEF RABBIS OF
ISRAEL, JERUSALEM, 2000

The Jewish religion is not "extrinsic" to us, but in a certain way is "intrinsic" to our own religion. With Judaism, therefore, we have a relationship which we do not have with any other religion. You are our dearly beloved brothers, and, in a certain way, it can be said that you are our elder brothers.

ADDRESS AT SYNAGOGUE IN ROME, 1986

Auschwitz, perhaps the most meaningful symbol of the *Holocaust of the Jewish people*, shows to what lengths a system constructed on principles of racial hatred and greed for power can go. To this day, Auschwitz does not cease to admonish, reminding us that *anti-Semitism is a great sin against humanity*, that all racial hatred inevitably leads to the trampling of human dignity.

CROSSING THE THRESHOLD OF HOPE

God of our fathers, you chose Abraham and his descendants to bring your Name to the Nations: we are deeply saddened by the behavior of those who in the course of history have caused these children of yours to suffer, and asking your forgiveness we wish to commit ourselves to genuine brotherhood with the people of the Covenant. We ask this through Christ our Lord. Amen.

PRAYER PLACED BY POPE JOHN PAUL II IN
THE WAILING WALL IN JERUSALEM, 2000

Let us build a new future in which there will be no more anti-Jewish feeling among Christians or anti-Christian feeling among Jews, but rather the mutual respect required of those who adore the one Creator and Lord, and look to Abraham as our common father in faith.

ADDRESS TO HOLOCAUST SURVIVORS
AT YAD VASHEM HOLOCAUST
MEMORIAL, 2000

We Christians joyfully recognize the religious values we have in common with Islam. Today I would like to repeat what I said to young Muslims some years ago in Casablanca: "We believe in the same God, the one God, the living God, the God who created the world and brings his creatures to their perfection."

ADDRESS TO MUSLIMS, 1999

The religiosity of Muslims deserves respect. It is impossible not to admire, for example, their *fidelity to prayer.* The image of believers in Allah who, without caring about time or place, fall to their knees and immerse themselves in prayer remains a model for all *those who invoke* the true God, in particular for those Christians who, having deserted their magnificent cathedrals, pray only a little or not at all.

CROSSING THE THRESHOLD OF HOPE

The example of people who live holy lives teaches us not only to practice mutual respect and understanding, but to be ourselves models of goodness, reconciliation and collaboration, across ethnic and religious boundaries, for the good of the whole country and for the greater glory of God.

MEETING WITH MUSLIM LEADERS,
ABUJA, NIGERIA, 1998

All the motives and expressions of the phenomenon of fundamentalism must be examined. The analysis of political, social and economic situations shows that the phenomenon is not only religious, but that in many cases religion is exploited for political ends or, indeed, to compensate for problems of a social and economic nature. There can be no really lasting response to the phenomenon of fundamentalism as long as the problems that create or sustain it are left unresolved.

MEETING WITH MUSLIMS, 1995

Shintoism, the traditional religion of Japan, affirms for example that all men are equally sons of God and that, because of this, all men are brothers. Moreover, in your religious tradition, you show a special sensitivity and appreciation for the harmony and beauty of nature, and you show a readiness to recognize there a revelation of God the Most High. . . . The many things that we hold in common impel us to unite ever more closely in friendship and brotherhood in the service of all humanity.

ADDRESS, ROME, 1979

The Catholic Church recognizes the truths that are contained in the religious traditions of India. This recognition makes true dialogue possible.

ADDRESS, MADRAS, INDIA, 1986

Religion is the enemy of exclusion and discrimination, of hatred and rivalry, of violence and conflict. . . . Religious belief and practice cannot be separated from the defense of the image of God in every human being.

ADDRESS WITH JEWISH, CHRISTIAN,
AND MUSLIM RELIGIOUS LEADERS, 2000

The Modern World

In the era of technology our life risks becoming always more anonymous and merely a function of the production process. In this way, man becomes incapable of enjoying the beauties of the Creator and to see in them the reflection of the face of God.

ADDRESS, ROME, 1998

When man turns his back on the Creator's plan, he provokes a disorder which has inevitable repercussions on the rest of the created order. If man is not at peace with God, then earth itself cannot be at peace.

THE ECOLOGICAL CRISIS, 1990

Only the human person, created in the image and likeness of God, is capable of raising a hymn of praise and thanksgiving to the Creator. The earth, with all its creatures, and the entire universe call on man to be their voice.

HOMILY, SAN ANTONIO, 1987

The exploration of both the micro and the macro cosmos, is a song to God's glory, which is reflected in everything in the universe.

JUBILEE ADDRESS TO MEN AND
WOMEN FROM THE WORLD OF
LEARNING, ROME, 2000

May academics and scientists always be aware of the lofty mission that Providence entrusts to them! Dear brothers and sisters, you too cooperate in this wonderful mission. In investigating the secrets of the cosmos and of the human being, you are drawing ever closer to the unfathomable mystery of God.

HOMILY AT MASS FOR UNIVERSITY
STUDENTS IN ROME, 2001

Science shines forth in all its value as a good capable of motivating our existence, as a great experience of freedom for truth, as a fundamental work of service. Through research each scientist grows as a human being and helps others to do likewise.

ADDRESS TO MEMBERS OF THE
PONTIFICAL ACADEMY OF SCIENCES,
2000

Science can purify religion from error and superstition; religion can purify science from idolatry and false absolutes. Each can draw the other into a wider world, a world in which both can flourish.

LETTER TO THE REVEREND GEORGE V.
COYNE, S.J., DIRECTOR OF THE
VATICAN OBSERVATORY, 1988

Halting the human cloning project is a moral duty which must also be translated into cultural, social and legislative terms. The progress of scientific research is not the same as the rise of scientific despotism.

MESSAGE FROM THE PONTIFICAL
ACADEMY FOR LIFE, 1997

At the level of human rights, the possibility of human cloning represents a violation of the two fundamental principles on which all human rights are based: the principle of equality among human beings and the principle of nondiscrimination.

MESSAGE FROM THE PONTIFICAL
ACADEMY FOR LIFE, 1997

An ever increasing number of scientists are becoming aware of their human responsibility and are convinced that there cannot be science without conscience. This fundamental thought is a positive and encouraging gain of our own time, which is better able to measure the limits of scientism, which one should take good care not to identify with science itself.

ADDRESS AT THE UNIVERSITY OF FRIBOURG, SWITZERLAND, 1984

The modern technological world can offer us many pleasures, many comforts of life. It can even offer us temporary escapes from life. But what the world can never offer is lasting joy and peace. These are the gifts which only the Holy Spirit can give.

SPEECH TO YOUTH, NEW ORLEANS, 1987

Remembering Pope John Paul II

I came for you. Now you have come to me. And I thank you.

SAID TO BE AMONG POPE JOHN PAUL
II'S LAST WORDS, ROME, APRIL 2, 2005

Pope John Paul II was unquestionably the most influential voice for morality and peace in the world during the last 100 years. His extraordinary gifts, his strong Catholic faith, and his experience of human tyranny and suffering in his native Poland all shaped him, and yet he was respected by men and women from every conceivable background across the world.

THE REVEREND BILLY GRAHAM

Pope John Paul II was, himself, an inspiration to millions of Americans, and to so many more throughout the world. We will always remember the humble, wise, and fearless priest who became one of history's great moral leaders. We're grateful to God for sending such a man, a son of Poland, who became the Bishop of Rome, and a hero for the ages.

GEORGE W. BUSH, U.S. PRESIDENT

Throughout a hard and often difficult life, he stood for social justice and on the side of the oppressed, whether as a young man facing the Nazi occupation in Poland or later in challenging the communist regime. He never wavered, never flinched, in the struggle for what he thought was good and right.

TONY BLAIR, BRITISH PRIME MINISTER

Quite apart from his role as a spiritual guide to more than a billion men, women, and children, he was a tireless advocate of peace, a true pioneer in interfaith dialogue, and a strong force for critical self-evaluation by the Church itself.

KOFI ANNAN, U.N. SECRETARY-GENERAL

Pope John Paul II was a man I held in high regard. His experience in Poland, then a communist country, and my own difficulties with communists gave us a common ground.

THE DALAI LAMA

[History] will retain the imprint and the memory of this exceptional sovereign pontiff, whose charisma, conviction, and compassion carried the evangelical message with unprecedented resonance on the international stage.

JACQUES CHIRAC, FRENCH PRESIDENT

[Without him] there would be no end of communism, or at least much later and the end would have been bloody.

LECH WALESA, LEADER OF POLAND'S SOLIDARITY MOVEMENT

His life was a long struggle against the lies employed to excuse evil. By combating the falsehoods of communism and proclaiming the true dignity of the individual, his was the moral force behind victory in the Cold War.

MARGARET THATCHER, FORMER BRITISH PRIME MINISTER

[Pope John Paul II's] devotion to his followers is a remarkable example to all of us.

MIKHAIL GORBACHEV, FORMER SOVIET
UNION LEADER

I have very warm recollections of meetings with the pope. He was wise, responsive, and open for dialogue.

VLADIMIR PUTIN, RUSSIAN PRESIDENT

It's a great loss for the whole world. We will always remember him as a great man, an advocate of justice and man of peace.

PERVEZ MUSHARRAF, PAKISTANI
PRESIDENT

We will miss him as a distinguished religious figure, who devoted his life to defending the values of peace, freedom, and equality. He defended the rights of Palestinians, their freedom and independence.

MAHMOUD ABBAS, PALESTINIAN
LEADER

Pope John Paul II was a man of peace and a friend of the Jewish people, who was familiar with the uniqueness of the Jewish people and who worked for an historic reconciliation between the peoples and for the establishment of diplomatic relations between Israel and the Vatican. . . . Yesterday, the world lost one of the most important leaders of our generation, whose great contribution to rapprochement and unity between peoples, understanding, and tolerance will be with us for many years.

ARIEL SHARON, ISRAELI PRIME
MINISTER

He advanced the ecumenical movement—he reached out to Jewish people, to those of the Islamic faith, and was also an inspiration to people of no faith at all.

JOHN HOWARD, AUSTRALIAN PRIME
MINISTER

Pope John Paul II wrote history. Through his work, and through his impressive personality, he changed our world.

GERHARD SCHRÖEDER, GERMAN
CHANCELLOR

Humanity will preserve an emotional memory of the tireless work of His Holiness John Paul II in favor of peace, justice, and solidarity among people.

FIDEL CASTRO, CUBAN PRESIDENT

We are all grateful for the tireless work and suffering that he bore incessantly against every form of totalitarianism, violence, oppression, and moral degradation in the name of the values of the Catholic Church that are also the supreme values of human dignity and solidarity.

SILVIO BERLUSCONI, ITALIAN PRIME MINISTER

Before my eyes is, in particular, the witness of Pope John Paul II. He leaves us a Church that is more courageous, freer, younger. A Church that, according to his teaching and example, looks with serenity to the past and is not afraid of the future.

POPE BENEDICT XVI'S FIRST MESSAGE, APRIL 20, 2005

Chronology of Pope John Paul II

May 18, 1920. Karol Józef Wojtyla is born in Wadowice, Poland.

September 15, 1926. Karol, nicknamed "Lolek," begins elementary school.

April 13, 1929. Karol's mother, Emilia, dies at the age of forty-five from kidney failure and congenital heart disease.

December 5, 1932. Karol's only brother, Edmund, a doctor, dies of scarlet fever that he contracted from a patient. He is twenty-six years old.

Fall, 1934. Karol begins performing in local theatrical productions.

May 3, 1938. Karol receives the sacrament of confirmation.

May 27, 1938. Karol, named class valedictorian, graduates from high school.

August 1938. Karol and his father move to Kraków where Karol begins his studies at Jagiellonian University.

July 1939. Karol completes compulsory military training with the American Legion.

September 1, 1939. Germany invades Poland and World War II begins.

November 1939. More than 180 professors from Jagiellonian University are arrested and deported to concentration camps. All formal studies are suspended. Karol begins underground studies and cultural activities.

September 1940. Karol begins working at a stone quarry.

February 18, 1941. Karol's father dies of a heart attack at the age of sixty-two.

Fall 1942. Karol begins underground seminary studies with the Archdiocese of Kraków.

November 1, 1946. Karol is ordained a priest.

November 15, 1946. Wojtyla begins graduate theological studies in Rome.

June 1948. Wojtyla is awarded his first doctorate degree.

July 1948. Having returned to Poland from his studies in Rome, Wojtyla begins his first parish assignment in Niegowiç, Poland.

March 17, 1949. Wojytla is assigned to St. Florian's parish in Kraków as assistant pastor.

January 1954. Wojtyla is awarded a second doctorate in theology from Jagiellonian Universtiy.

October 1954. Wojtyla joins the philosophy department of the Catholic University of Lublin, Poland.

December 1, 1956. Wojtyla is appointed to the Chair of Ethics at the Catholic University of Lublin.

July 4, 1958. Wojtyla is named auxiliary bishop of Kraków by Pope Pius XII. At thirty-eight years of age, he is the youngest bishop in Poland.

January 1960. Wojtyla's book *Love and Responsibility* is published.

October 1962. Vatican II opens. Wojtyla participates in all four sessions.

December 30, 1963. Wojtyla is named Archbishop of Kraków by Pope Paul VI.

June 28, 1967. Pope Paul VI makes Wojtyla a Cardinal.

Fall 1969. Wojtyla travels through Canada and the United States. He establishes the archdiocesan Institute of Family studies and participates in the international Synod of Bishops in Rome.

1969. Wojtyla's *Person and Act*, a major philosophical work, is published.

1970. Wojtyla publishes a guide to the documents of Vatican II entitled "Sources of Renewal."

February 1973. Wojtyla represents the Polish Church at the International Eucharistic Conference in Melbourne, Australia.

August 6, 1978. Pope Paul VI dies.

August 25, 1978. Albino Luciani is elected Pope. John Paul I dies on September 29.

October 16, 1978. Wojtyla is elected Pope and takes the name John Paul II.

1979. Pope John Paul II visits the Dominican Republic, Mexico, Poland, Ireland, the United States, and Turkey.

1980 to 2004. Pope John Paul II makes pastoral visits to Italy and to another 123 countries.

May 13, 1981. Pope John Paul II is shot in St. Peter's Square by Mehmet Ali Agca.

August 1985. Pope John Paul II addresses 80,000 young Muslims in Casablanca.

April 1986. Pope John Paul II addresses the Roman Jewish community at the Synagogue of Rome.

October 1986. Pope John Paul II hosts World Day of Prayer for Peace in Assisi, an ecumenical gathering that brings world religious leaders together.

December 1989. Pope John Paul II meets with Russian President Mikhail Gorbachev at the Vatican.

January 1991. Pope John Paul II writes letters to George Bush and to Saddam Hussein urging a peaceful resolution to the crisis in the Persian Gulf.

March 25, 1994. Pope John Paul II's eleventh encyclical, *Evangelium Vitae* is published.

April 1994. Pope John Paul II fractures his leg and undergoes hip replacement surgery.

October 1994. Pope John Paul II's book *Crossing the Threshold of Hope* is published.

January 1995. Pope John Paul II says Mass before an estimated five million people for the closing of the fifth international World Youth Day in Manila.

October 1995. Pope John Paul II addresses the 50th meeting of the UN General Assembly.

November 1996. Pope John Paul II's memoir, *Gift and Mystery* is published.

January 1998. Pope John Paul II makes his first pilgrimage to Cuba.

April 26, 1999. Pope John Paul II meets with the Minister of Foreign Affairs of Israel, Ariel Sharon.

December 24, 1999. Pope John Paul II opens the Holy Door of St. Peter's Basilica and begins the Great Jubilee of the Year 2000.

March 2000. Pope John Paul II in his Jubilee Pilgrimage visits the Holy Land.

April 2002. Pope John Paul II summons U.S. cardinals to the Vatican to address sex abuse scandal.

May 2003. Vatican confirms that Pope John Paul II has Parkinson's disease.

June 2003. Pope John Paul II makes his 100th trip abroad, visiting Croatia.

October 2003. Pope John Paul II celebrates the 25th anniversary of his election as pope.

September 2004. Pope John Paul II's second volume of memoirs, *Rise, Let Us Be On Our Way* is published.

February 2005. Pope John Paul II is rushed to the hospital with influenza and difficulties breathing. He returns to the hospital later in the month and a tracheotomy is performed.

March 2005. Pope John Paul II's book *Memory and Identity: Conversations at the Dawn of a Millennium* is published.

April 2, 2005. Pope John Paul II dies at the age of 84.